Misery Prefigured

CRAB ORCHARD AWARD SERIES IN

Misery Prefigured

J. ALLYN ROSSER

Crab Orchard Review

& Southern Illinois University Press

Carbondale and Edwardsville

Printed in the United States of America

04   03   02   01   4   3   2   1

The Crab Orchard Award Series in Poetry is a joint publishing
venture of Southern Illinois University Press and *Crab Orchard Review.*
This series has been made possible by the generous support of the Office
of the President of Southern Illinois University and the Office of the
Vice Chancellor for Academic Affairs and Provost at Southern Illinois
University Carbondale.

Crab Orchard Award Series in Poetry Editor: Jon Tribble
Judge for 2000: Rodney Jones

Text design by Erin Kirk New

Library of Congress Cataloging-in-Publication Data

Rosser, J. Allyn (Jill Allyn), [date]
Misery prefigured / J. Allyn Rosser.
p. cm. — (Crab Orchard award series in poetry)
I. Title. II. Series.
PS3568.O8466 M57 2001
811'.54—dc21   00-059566
ISBN 0-8093-2383-4 (alk. paper)

Even if memory could retain a true impression, we must perceive it as we do a dancing partner in a zebra shirt strobed with black light.

—Sofía Gómez de Huesca, *The Life That Leads You*

To be literally incapable of motion at last, that must be something! My mind swoons when I think of it. And mute into the bargain! And perhaps as deaf as a post! And who knows as blind as a bat! And as likely as not your memory a blank! And just enough brain intact to allow you to exult! And to dread death like a regeneration.

—Samuel Beckett, *Molloy*

You are not the same people who left that station
Or who will arrive at any terminus,
While the narrowing rails slide together behind you . . .

—T. S. Eliot, "The Dry Salvages"

Contents

Acknowledgments

The author would like to thank the editors of the following journals and anthologies in which poems in this book previously appeared (sometimes in different form):

The Boston Phoenix Literary Section—"Reading at the Y"
The Georgia Review—"Beckett Dead Imagine," "The Brain of the World," "The Cry," "Heart to India," "Renouncing the Tower," and "Square Dance, Fourth Grade"
The Gettysburg Review—"Composite" and "Sole Blessing"
Michigan Quarterly Review—"Delayed Response" and "Late Elvis"
New England Review—"Suburban Report" and "Realism"
The Ohio Review—"North Jersey Farmland, Vile Mood"
Ontario Review—"The Next Stop Stopping"
Ploughshares—"Patience Is a Virtue"
Poetry—"Before the Sickness Is Official," "Buffalo Bayou," "Coming Your Way," "Deep Pond at Dusk in Heavy Rain Against Pines," "Eschatology of the Lexicon," "Late Letter," "Lover Release Agreement," "Much Later," "Raven," *"Sea and Rain,"* "Sugar Dada," and "The Sum Contradiction of Our Shades"
Slate—"Missing Person"
Third Coast—"Password"

"The Cry" was reprinted in *The 1997 Pushcart Prize XXI.*

"Sea and Rain" was reprinted in *A Visit to the Gallery,* published by the University of Michigan Art Museum.

"North Jersey Farmland, Vile Mood" and "Realism" were reprinted in the *1995/1996 Anthology of Magazine Verse & Yearbook of American Poetry.*

Thanks also to the National Endowment for the Arts and to Mark Cox, Rodney Jones, and the late Stanley Lindberg.

One

Sole Blessing

To say *screw them*, to be screw-them
bent on one thing all but lost,
one music or mystery,
beyond all the necessary
incidental snaggings of the heart;

to train the whole soul's beam
on a solitary hill, or on it
a special kind of rock or creeper;
to be sated just by saxophone;
to want nothing but your eyes

lifelong to study Scottish otters:
the snub, slippery-whiskered snout;
the way they intertwine in threes
at play, indistinguishably bound,
long sleek backs submerging away . . .

To make of this your being's aim,
its joy, and know by pulse and viscus
the word *joy*. No gifts but thine
to thyself: thou canst, if thou list,
single out, make good, one wish.

This from the dumb lips of an old god
who with one endless, misty hand
holds out to us too much to love,
and with the other—crooked-fingered,
crazed with veins—some nights and days.

Square Dance, Fourth Grade

We just were not ready for this.
Certainly not the freckled boys
with quick tight frowns at once
acquired and instinctive; not the girls,
dead against using the gym
for dancing, against a formal celebration
of otherness—as if we enjoyed it!—
when the natural impulse was to
whack the other in the head
with a book or anything handy
that wasn't our actual hand,
an act of preservation both
direct and distant, like whirling
tops that bump and cringe away . . .

Did we sense misery prefigured
in stepping forward and back,
the coupling chant of dosey-do?
And in the fiddle, ridiculous
instrument with giggle and slide,
resembling our voices at recess?
I hated grasping any boy's hand,
sweaty and rough—more *real* than mine—
the way the tongue revolts against
a slab of beef tongue: horror in touching
what the thing touching is.

We learned to manage holding hands
by gloving ourselves in darkness,
in theaters and parked cars;
but then the soul, too, revealed
twin horrors. There was shame
sewn into the lining of loneliness.
Or there was intimacy: the more
we bared our souls, the more they
shrank or howled, drew back in mists.
Some love withheld might have helped,
like highbeams lowered in a fog.
But to be forced to merge, and still
feel separate and blind and cold!
Then to attend love's swearing-in,
the all-night argument, the souls'
first formal, chilling introduction —
like the film my sister loved to watch,
Frankenstein Meets the Wolfman —
matched agonies of recognition,
evenly monstrous, haunted, but haunting
mostly for the mutual strangulation
it ended with: hollow-eyed, perfunctory.
Believe me, we could never have been
ready for this, to see up close in each
sweet ache, each reaching out to passion
the terrible image, undarkenable,
of passion wanting.

Resurfaced

At the end of a long paycheck this archaeologist
walked up. Did digs, spelunked. Land's End eyes.
I was standing starving beside the cheese cubes
because it was my job to be dithered at
fanatically all day by well-fed people
who didn't know how hungry I was.
The *Welcome* part of the convention banner
was a little askew, okay for a Ramada gig,
but this was Hyatt, my reputation at stake.
I listened, not reaching for a single cube.
I am only that polite when I don't want to be.
You just have to accept that about me,
I told my first husband, then my second.
Eventually he quit dithering and
(probably rehearsing the day's lecture)
started describing this nomadic tribe who dwelt
in cliffy regions of Albania, and the persons
among this people who would laboriously
hew footholds into the loftiest cliffs,
there being no other access to the top;
they'd chisel and hack and chop rock
just to get up there, then solitarily carve
their large meaning—abstract or animal—
and then just as painstakingly shave off
every last foothold on their way down.
Maybe Afghanistan. So you could see the thing,
but never get close enough to mess with it.
I stood there shifting my spike heels
on the starprinted ballroom carpet,
recalling the look on my first's face when I left,
stony and pale, as though someone had
not only deepened his pained expression
but erased some features too, and thinking that still
was not enough. Let me tell you,
it hadn't been easy getting under his skin

and it was no picnic getting back out.
He mentioned the tribe's name twice
but my things were in another wing
of the hotel, twenty flights up,
so I didn't record it—I'm not one of those
types who carries a pen, you just have
to accept that about me, but I do carry
that look everywhere, and the way
it inspired me to refuse all the money
I had coming—plenty! On top of everything
I'd said and kept from saying
I knew that would cut him good
and prevent anyone from ever
getting up there as high with him
as I had. It's true I'm only generous
when I'm hungry for something,
but I'm honest. And I can assure you
that he left the reverse of a mark on me;
some men just don't know when to quit;
they wind up resurfacing women like marble
when they want to rough them up.
The archaeologist went off to give his talk
and the room thinned out a bit.
I piled one of those little plates so high
with toothpicked cubes, carefully
impaling them pick over pick,
that the server behind the immaculate cloth
raised both eyebrows, which I could have
had him fired for, but didn't. What I want
is for you to see how unmarked I am.
By the time the archaeologist came back
for me, I had eaten every inch of that cheese
and wiped the plate until it gleamed.

Voodoo That You Do

He wasn't just another one with another one.
This one's words you cradled violently
between your hands, legs, years until they
broke, scalded, clanged off down the hall.
He was ominously unmusical, dressed.
You should have guessed, could not have known.
His greeting caused Canada geese to unvee,
lower themselves.
Naturally, ironically, you could hardly help but
help him hurt you, and like a sister,
valet, idiot, you'd have waited
to displease him until he dropped off the key,
went to sleep, and though by that time you'd have
gladly sent him packing, sewn
his lips to your cheek,
he was suddenly, with plenty of warning, gone,
arching his absent back against your heart, buttocks,
well.
You had to laugh a little, unsuccessfully,
a lot before you could run with abandon,
   weep with abandon, sleep with abandon,
marry, have children with, and divorce abandon
so that when he returned you'd be ready;
so that when he assured you in the flesh, by the flesh and
   for (you would know this) the flesh
that he was never always not coming back
and having come back solely to tell you this
and to keep coming around in waves
like a series of fire drills before leaving town,
no explanation, you flat—
you would have learned not to quit
being ready for that.

Quest of the Prell

We were functioning as one; it was a flying dream.
I was holding his hand, he mine. I hadn't yet glimpsed
his face (when you're flying you don't care).
Sand-hued gazelles sipped at a green lagoon,
and there was no question but that we both needed
to get closer;
                        descending, found instead a playground
beside a green pond, no, massive bottle of Prell Shampoo,
like the one in the commercial where a man's hand drops
a pearl, which slowly sinks through the green murk,
to show how thick the murk must be to slow the pearl.
And he sighed with a look I knew from somewhere,
as if he'd said *What's wrong?* and I'd answered *Nothing*
unconvincingly—a tired, determined look,
suggesting this was yet another test
of love. His quest: to swim the Prell.
What's worse, I think I seemed to want him to;
and woke in horror, though not sure whose.
Is this what the male psyche thinks it's up against
in a relationship (the very word ungainly)
with a woman, wummin, womyn,
dividing his energies among the recycled
merry-go-round arguments, and manning
the unbalanced swingset of romance,
trying to swing as she swings,
at the same velocity and height,
so as to keep everything even
between them? Then off to navigate
her jungle gym without getting to the top
first, trying not to put his foot down
on hers, her career, her herness,
or lose his tender grip on her notion
of what their life could be?

Oh, must he seesaw with her endlessly
on that creaking, warped emery board
laid across the moat of her past,
swirling with such desires as she herself
can hardly see, with prehistorically
huge appetites and indiscriminate teeth?

Not to say it isn't terrifying on the woman's end
of things, like going down the slide backwards
sans underwear, and which will it be this time
at bottom: the burning sands of his indifference;
the asphalt of disdain; or will he laughing catch her up?

This all sounds so fifties, I know, the Prell,
the desire to be caught, but it was his look
that left me shaking. I've seen it on every lover
and husband of every last one of my women friends,
and now on you—though it wasn't your face
really; let's not forget this was a dream—
inheriting that look from every man regarding
every woman, that awful look of resignation
to face the rich green goo of her being;
the hero hardily willing to hold his breath
grimaceless, refrain from muttering *Oh, swell,*
and blindly dive to retrieve that cultured pearl,
dropped long ago by an unknown man's
unthinking hand (just to prove a point)
into the opaque murk of her self, her very *elle;*
into the thick, slick, deep, man-handled,
bottled-up, unreal green of her Prell.

As she heroically must stand there
helpless, watching him.

Deep Pond at Dusk in Heavy Rain Against Pines

I come back inside breathless I say
honey beside this green
no other green *is*

barkmoss and hemlocks and all
the shaded lawns of late May
garish
in comparison

    stick your face in a mint plant
    you say
    that's green

no I'm telling you
honey Robinhood's eyes
even if they were green
as the eyes of that boy
I met when I was thirteen
with new hungers
under the trees
would seem pale
beside the utterness
of this
you should see
the sky leaning down
almost into it
gray with envy
and tension building
in the water's surface
wild curving current patterns
and sharp rainpoints sharp
sharp the pines stand back
waiting for something
to give
nothing gives

meanwhile the wind raking
and raking at this essence
the naked eye despairs of

green like deep breathing
just after a long sleep
and soft jazz in the next room

you meanwhile
shaking your head slightly
with that dismissive laugh

but honey (I don't say)
I would leave even you
for a life of this color

The Sum Contradiction of Our Shades

This morning holding the book
of Turner plates
you would never get for me
though every year I asked

      reading over and over how
      for four hours in a severe storm
      Turner pitched madly
      lashed to the mast of a boat

staring at this book
as at yet another example
of your strangely attractive disdain
for what I loved most

      lashed to the mast of a boat he knew
      might never make it back

wondering why I should have needed you
or the backdrop of your shocked face
to see the decent sense
my past had made of me

      to know the force of that storm
      from being tossed
      defenseless against it

and thinking about our wreckage
I happen to look up from *Storm at Sea*
to see Madame Cézanne leaning slightly
in the print tacked up on the door
I mostly now keep closed

Madame Cézanne in a Red Armchair
in which Rilke identified
the first and only
really red chair ever

and it occurs to me
I must have wanted you
to be set so against me
your rages could not be contained
I must have wanted you that way
to verify whatever brightness
I embodied

    the way Cézanne wanted Madame
    in that chair
    for the chair
    so clearly a color
    she was against
    yet in her lips and fingers
    barely visible traces
    sharpening the contrast

I want to tell you I understand
now I see now
the faint traces of me
in you
were what nearly killed us both

    just as Turner's eyes
    must have teared slightly
    their own salt water
    in the slicing salt wind

though when I speak to you now
it must be from the life I hold
under the waters of this one
the life I can no longer afford
to offer blood to

seeing again that tension
that exact diagonal
of sea against light
body against spirit

can't I said to you that time
and   *don't*

   to watch the whipped foam
   and seaspray turn all the world
   around to a roiling flashing dark
   leaving the light inside him
   more purely manifest

but my voice wouldn't carry
as if I were speaking from underwater
from under another tongue
maybe yours   less lucid

   Soapsuds and whitewash
   the critics sneered
   and Turner shrugged
   I wonder he said mildly

what to do with these old stills
tinted weirdly submarine
that surface and again
surface like those bobbling
messages in a water-filled
Magic Eight-Ball

   I wonder what they think the sea's like
   I wish they'd been in it

you grimacing you smiling you
standing or floating in the blue room
of that house we couldn't keep
a darker blue churning in your eyes
a bluish cast to the skin along your jaw
and we are not speaking for hours together

for four hours in a severe

not speaking

Madame's lips closed
over something
the shadows at each temple
like bruises

and everything gone blue
traces even in the moon
my own lips
when I try now to sing
myself having really
so little to do with such a color
which the sum contradiction
of all our shades has become
all of it that hue
behind my back

lashed

Composite

When he forced his first entry there,
I fought. He struck me: my mistake.
Of course I knew it wasn't fair,
   and kept my small chin up.
He brought stupid balloons and cake
I didn't want, but I stayed
   if only to clean up.
I was a child. I obeyed.

Later he tried to leave. I bound him
(by then his leaving hurt me too):
I made my muscles close around him.
   He showed some surprise.
My embrace made him fiercer to go.
The sun reared twice and twice fell down
   as he struggled to rise.
Strong and twenty, I held on.

He once said I was what they'd win
that night, jacks wild, keeping score
on napkins they pressed bills between.
   Such thick smoke sprawled
among them, if Truth walked in the door
she would to them have seemed untrue.
   I said so. They all roared.
Being a woman, I withdrew.

When he came wanting me again,
I stood my ground. I'd seen the pit
well camouflaged by other men.
   My warning went unheard,
for he was busy with his wit
and slipped. And though by then he hung
   for life on my least word,
I was a lady, and I held my tongue.

Renouncing the Tower

May God be praised for woman
That gives up all her mind . . .
   —W. B. Yeats

That is no monument for bright women. Men
And witches locked us there when we'd excelled
Too well: Danaë's eyes and chiseled chin;
Rumpelstiltskin's miller's daughter, skilled
To a fault in spinning. Even our best gave in:
Cleopatra had her own slaves build
Her tower (tomb). Shalott walked out, undid
The spell; gullible, believed she'd die. And did.

And who can blame them? From such eminence,
Man had no choice but to look down—thumping
Bible or cane, declaiming sentiments
From certain heights of Yes and No, stomping
Back and forth between the battlements
Intoning *right/wrong, black/white,* and dumping
In-betweens out back at night. Peeing
Yellow, after all. Mere human being.

Nope, it's not our kind of place, this glorified
Flagpole made for pacing, squinting, ranting,
Disapproving the rank decade: upright
Finger insisting, delineating, expounding
The one way. Maybe linear is *not* right.
Solipsism is not insight abounding.
So take my halo—but leave the golden hair,
And I'll still let it down. But not from there.

Two

Coming Your Way

A woman walks, absorbed in the air
of her ill fortune, absorbing
the clean breeze in the sunlight
of a small town, seeing what she sees
through the lens of what she's seen before,
as through glasses custom-made
for someone else. For someone else,
surely, because the events
that brought her here didn't suit her
in temperament, conditioning, appetite.
Was it her *fault* she'd been so unhappy?
Were the events, the people, so bad?
Think of the results of good perfume
at the wrong time; the bitter mouthwash
of wine after a glass of milk.

Too bad if our schedules keep us
up late, coffee in our cups,
when we like to turn in early.
Or force us to commute in bad traffic,
in bad air, the first and last hours
of daylight, small birds flying
out of focus on the flat white sky
as we idle and surge and idle, staring
at the changeless billboards and exit signs
we can never get to in time,
causing us to hate our jobs
and speak tensely to our loved ones,
who perhaps love us
too irritatingly well, too calmly . . .

We adjust as we can to what nears us.
We turn, and turn, like leafy plants
to the sun of our circumstance,
hardly noticing the gradual alterations
to our tastes in music, recreation,
food, even forms of intimacy.
Women who live together align cycles.
Men who drink together every week
begin to laugh in roughly the same way:
the new half-scornful laugh
that alienates an office superior
or close friend, or a wife.

And now this woman whose good intentions
have soured through bad alloys
of companionship, diet, occupation—
she is new in town and is looking around
mistrustfully, but with a shred of hope
as fine as the unraveled strand of hair
that lifts and falls, troubling her cheek
as she walks slowly but steadily
across the green, heading for this very spot.

She will turn to one of us
and one of us will turn to her
or away. Look at your blank faces!
Why are we all gathered here
if not to couple souls on earth?
Who among us can convert
without a single touch
the sour in her thwarted self
to sweet? You? You?

Song

You've never heard the song
you've heard of for so long.
Something like it plays along
the lips of your friend's friend
you never get to see, like the word
love on the lips of a bad actor,
and it wavers like coiled smoke
on the steps leading to stage left
where it was just heard in a club
beside a diner called the Déjà-Vous,
whether joke or mistake
you can't tell, the town being
so small, not yours, not
far, but by the time you arrive
out of breath in a too-thin coat,
having forgotten your watch, and
God, even your wallet, you find
the club owner has skipped town,
leaving the business to the owner
of the D-V who carries you a cup
of okay coffee and only smiles
a negative when you ask him
for change for the jukebox.
That song is not there on it.
You count on your rosary of
if only's, to stay calm:
if you'd only been bold enough
to pester people, to collar
the proprietor of the last store
stocking LPs before it folded,
to ask around perpetually,
who sang it who wrote it won't
you just please make me a tape?
I'll provide the blank cassette
you could have said, no, here's

my heart, put it right there,
I'll erase everything else,
I'll be your blank, *I'll be*
your blank!

How much for the coffee.

You couldn't, any more
than they could have sung it
past a few shaky, tuneless bars.
Yet you always nod happily when
they speak of it, your eyes
distant, your lips slightly open
as if to sing it for them.

Suburban Report

In the suburbs of New Jersey, some twenty miles
from Forked River, not far from Oyster Creek
and several other sites for nuclear plants
whose outlandish open-mouthed shapes
already resemble ancient ruins,
we are still sweeping dirt from the sidewalks.
We are watering the perennials, raking gravel,
and stooping to pick up stray leaves.
We continue the tradition of yard sales.
On garbage night, when the youngest children
have gone to sleep, we gather on the curb
to fold our arms and speak in low tones.

Out here in the suburbs we're getting things
in order, we're learning to look calm;
when the final flash goes off
at least we can afford to be clean,
we can be on top of things: bills paid,
clothes pressed, hemlines straight.
Sometimes we think wanly of Pompeii
and the fame accorded charred relics;
or we think of the Guanajuato mummies,
their cold thin cheeks and lips still holding taut
to shape the ancient O, the skulls
outlined beneath them mouthing *cheese*.

Eschatology of the Lexicon

They come down to us
rounding the corners of centuries
at an innocent jog, shedding letters
and most of the grand old meanings
to take on the sleek new hide
our day demands, a snappier
nap that can repel the stare
of a rather less tactful sun;

they come down to us com-
pounding, bounding in idiot
joy, they come with that trustful
tired old mutt look, that soft woof,
warm doggie sigh on the knee,
hoping for what? Some reason,
no doubt, to continue sounding.
Give me one good reason,

they come down to us saying,
as if we could have one without them.

Decreator

You could say this man beats God
for strength. At least for strength of will.
Because what he will do is just what
God could not bring himself quite to,
though a few times he came close.

cold spring water, whiff of rose

He will awe more, have more fame
than anyone in his hour,
though very few will know his name.
Perhaps the ones who do will be knocked
unconscious. Otherwise they'd stop him.

whorl of bat's ear, tongue of robin

We will not read his journals, know
his heart, though we'll assume he lived
unloved. Yet this will not be true.
Nor did she dump him, or disappear.
Or die, although he knew she would.

blind rapture, being understood

Will that be why? The energy
of pulse and growth, thought and urge
destined to a corpse; memory
to rot along with brain, a legacy
of nothing for no good reason?

mote of pollen, change of season

We will not hear his eighth-grade tutor
say he'd seen it coming, his prom date's
tale of how awkwardly he wooed her—
the documentary will not be made.
Not one obit will give him credit.

the first "I love you" and how she said it

Here, too, he'll supersede his Maker
in not insisting we record
and venerate his acts—plague or
drought or flood or risen dead.
Vainglory will not drive this man.

water, rock, windprints in the sand

And if it be a woman, if I'm
wrong, a woman whose command
will stop, or unfulfill, our time;
a woman and upon me proved,
know this: she will have known this man.

Much Later

Small children ask the right questions,
but who has time? *Later. Some day.*
Besides, they can't understand. Won't.
   Once grown,
gone. Then all those pat becauses
you slicked down on their glossy heads
   bounce back
in cowlicks of your own.

Now that you have time to pick up
after yourself and linger over
boxes in the marital attic,
   you stumble
on tough little kernels of wisdom,
risible carrots and peas, black
   with neglect.
They rattle around in the dark.

Ellipses and loose ends have undone you,
snaking dryly down important halls
on the heels of your tall children.
   Options blink
and digitize in birthday watches,
write themselves out of life-
   long contracts
you had meant to explain.

You wish someone would explain.
When the children come home they look
knowing. You'd like to ask how
   they manage
to forget what's wrong, to stay busy.
Instead you start explaining everything.
   They nod, smile.
They don't remember asking you.

You Are Here ●

Today the newsstand's twenty tiers
are longer than when last you looked,
thronging with panics, longings explained
and tracked, rationalized, media-forgiven:
a garden of magazines affordably displays
in color all you don't know anything about.
Art in Tunisia. Ventriloquist Today.
Your ignorance blooms like a thistle
with barbs and seeds that will fill the yard
with more thistles, barbs and seeds
if you don't thumb through something now, get this,
how to stuff a zebra, baste a dirndl waist,
skin an eggplant. A piece on how to roast a puffin
(Irish Times) nestles beside *Birder's Digest.*
Look, this magazine tells all about the other
magazines. *Etymology Now* says *magazine*
means "arsenal." Every hour you don't destroy
the wasps, their attic nests grow bigger, rustle louder.
Dump your "Sump Pump Blues" in *Plumber's Almanac.*
Every night you reach for the remote
and not that college-vintage Proust in French,
your skills in comprehension will diminish
by a hair, *par un cheveu. un cil?* Forget it.
"Feng Shui for Agoraphobes" in *Interior Design.*
Every day you don't worry about your husband
driving on the slick highway/loving someone else
he becomes more likely to skid/meet her
or you get less resilient, less able to handle
the collision/collusion when it happens
as it must, cf. *Nostra Damus Review. Cat Psychiatry.*
"Bankruptcy for Everyone" in *Money Talks.*
Each time your eyes slink from columns on Kosovo,
the situation there gets more complex.
Here is how to attract deer, how to repel them,
How to Make Your Own Sun Screen.

During the hour when your back is turned,
it stoops a fraction more. *Journal of Myth
and Meaning. Metaphysics Review.* Every leaf
you don't turn over turns the unlived life
to compost you can't use. The blanks
on the form you don't fill out get longer,
underscore your every abandoned reflection
until the pages of your diary are only lines
flat-lining, soon the lines you make yourself
aren't even straight but weakly inked and palsied,
sloping, soon the shadows longer than the figures,
soon the echo clearer than the voice,
the ink gone dry, the pen ungripped, let fall,
soon just scratches, clawmarks, soon you only think
you're making even those.

Patience Is a Virtue

When something irks you, let your anger build—
Don't spend it in a temporary snit.
Don't leave your smallest passion unfulfilled.

"Let bygones be bygones," say the weak-willed.
Nah. Watch where a bygone goes, and bottle it.
Appreciate your anger. Let it build

Vast *caves* of vintage rage, best when chilled.
Invest in every wrong and market it.
Don't leave your smallest passion unfulfilled.

If Noah annoyed you while he hammered and drilled
His ark, stay calm. Wait till the varnish has set
To strike the match. Let your anger build.

Say the boss takes credit for work you billed,
Then wins an award. Act thrilled. *Wait.* Then quit
When he's sick. Don't leave that passion unfulfilled.

Just keep your minefields mummed and daffodilled.
If someone dots your lawn with his dog's shit,
Lie low in it. Let your anger build.
Let your anger build. Let it build.

Phase 3: Final Interview, a Few Last Questions

If a stranger getting on a train you're leaving
makes as if to put his cigarette out in your eye,
do you let the doors close behind you with sorrow
for what some woman must have done to his life
or do you just hate him *hate* him
or do you hate yourself for letting him make you
hate him? Is this one of those hatreds
you're allowed to have, that you can justify?
Do you shield your eyes on the next platform
or do you smile valiantly, chin up, unsquinting?

If you know the words to a song you hear sung
uncertainly on the street at dusk by a stranger,
is it right to sing along, is it an invasion
or an obligation to connect, only connect,
even if he's wearing spurs and chains
and aims a spurt of spittle at your foot?
If some of your best friends wear chains,
should you mention it? With how wide a smile?
Should you invite him home to play the record,
or in the next world will you regret it,
or worse, regret it if you don't, why worse,
or in the next world is there no regret?
No looking back? No next world?

If a butler in the familiar and shabby livery
of someone else's trouble brings you a message
on a silver plate—and stands waiting—
should you fling it into the fire unread?
Should you excuse yourself and leave by the back door,
should you read it and swallow the return
address, and murder the butler, and leave
with too little money to make it back in case
the desire to help should ever seize you again?
It's not important, you virtually already
have the job but we'd still like to know.

Reading at the Y

He'd been big, one of the awesome three.
We were glad to see him in good health,
clear-eyed, and still with so much hair.
Nevertheless, I turned to my friend, saying
This reading could be as a death to us.
And he, agreeing, spake back: *Let him not
have become a fatuous drunk.*
And we were afraid.
Because we loved what we knew of God's work,
we needed at the very least to like him,

the brevity of whose name no longer struck us
as mysterious: one letter more than Ai,
one less than Cher.
He looked at us as if to memorize our eyes,
then cleared his throat, like the shattering
of a glass down the dark hall. He lifted up
a book we had not seen and read in a voice
that seemed to smooth the corners of the room;
and the microphone, stooped with the boredom
of its century and clogged with lesser expression,

became functional once more, and radiant.
And his words were well pronounced and true.
And his words must have leaked sweetly
out of windows into the honking, failed city.
And my friend looked to me and I to him
with soothed eyes.
And when it was done, we felt meaning settle
softly on us like a mantle on the shoulders of one
who must go into the night unfed, unshod,
and find the child wandered off, and feed and clothe him.

Three

Heart to India

(Volume 14 of the *Encyclopedia Americana*)

Here without you, where mere pages impart
The separation of hussy from husband, hate
From hurt, immortal soul from incarnate,
India ink, indelible . . . Just think! My heart
Sails after simple facts, without a stray
Thought for safe return (just browsing, it murmurs)
Seeking the fastest possible passage away
From heartsick, where it had been, to somewhere
In a book where Heaven and I can coexist
Without you. —Hell, I only meant to say
You're missed. It's just that one's sole heart insists
On traveling in purdah, peeking from veils
Of vermilion, as if its own red spice were not
Itself exotic, not the treasure sought.

Second Story, Old Snow

Just now I stood, revising winter daylight,
having moved so only air was there to see:
stood at my window in the snowless white light,
lightly, like a tall idea, pleased to be alone,
to look unsquinting into unstinted pallor
swaying, as if hanging by a thread

. . . slipped into looking out your window
some dozen years ago, second-story bedroom.
Snow was coming down hard back then,
down soft. You were muffled in demi-sleep,
saying something that was just nothing,
not What is it?, not Come back to bed,
just palping the cloud-colored quilt, uttering
translated breath, airy preverbal reachings
to let me know you were alone, almost
awake.
         Shoo! I'm awake now, nothing
between us now but a little bitterness,
like the last second before the lozenge
disintegrates, turns to tongue. It was
your window, your house. To you I was
as a half-freed fly to a tired spider out of silk,
content just to feel the old web still holding.
This thought leaks like a cold draft
between these panes and those, conflating
old snow and now's *no-snow—no's now, nos-*
talgia nosferatu nosotros—what? shoo!
the mind buzzing, to shake free.

Do our memories hold us so casually?
Are we bound to the world by memory alone,
such that even our freshest-feeling thoughts
attach to the oldest strands in the weft,
selvage to selvage? To think there is nothing new
to think. That would have been your favorite line.
To think all thought is a dried powder,
the same old stuff needing a little fresh spit
to make it stick. To drape its intermittent
glimmer of sense once more, twice more
between the physical and the dreamt,
plus one, minus one, come to nothing, to bed?

Do spiders ever eat their webs in desperation?

What I liked most about you was the notion
that you didn't need me. You had me going.

Shoo! You neural smudge, you failed visitation.
It is not snowing now. Not snowing now.
Was that blessed sense at the window
of needing no one ever at all
too thin a thread to hang by?
So how come you, of all beloveds least,
and least mine, dead now these years,
wake now full strength here, while I
almost not, I pale, I weightless, snowlike
I falling up into the nearly invisible sky now
wound within this freshfelt newspun true one?

Rods and R.

Twenty years ago she disappeared, R. did.
I'm glad, though I loved her utterably
when she was a friend in front of me, crazy laugh,
crazy gaze, toe-tapping even at her calmest—
but how I love her now, it's beyond me,
luminously immense my love, my thrill in her
unzipcodable immanence. Picture her
in the thousand lives she may be living,
counting rubles perched on a windowsill
in Arles, or beneath a tattered sail on choppy
water with lots of crazy hair flying in her eyes
that can't spot me, the sun dashing
her image and reforming it like a wave
after each crash resurgent, regathering.
If I could see her now, across the table,
she'd just be here. *So R., I'd say, R.,*
how are you? I'd use her full name
and that would help to ruin everything,
not a pretty or fitting one. Her half-
efforts to be one of us always missed
the mark she left us making. Her other friends
still swivel distractedly toward her absence.
Not me. I fancy her drifting in and out
of unsatisfactory embraces like a seahorse,
her posture of indifference betrayed by that
ghostly tail curled in permanent longing.
I get a better look at her now than I did.
You see more keenly from the distant rim.
The farther you get from the center
of the eyeball, the more rods there are, and rods
can see things cones get in the way of.
Rods line up like a forest of lodgepole pine
to frame the impossible under poor conditions,
when the night collapses in shadow. What
is that on the unmooned owlful slope,

the silver movement five yards west of your glance?
Look head-on at that comet and it's gone.
Damn the cones, dim the facts, the lights,
the impulse to turn and see what you know you
have seen. Lot's wife saw before turning, then
not a jot. Salt sifted first past her eyes, dried them,
then down her twisted torso, filling her swiftly
like the last grains of hourglass. Even Eurydice
may not have been lost to a real hell, only
the land of cones, full frontal mundanity.
       The instant of his looking.
If you want to see me, darling, look away.
If you must be emblazoned on my inmost retina,
leave now. Cleave unto the music down the street,
stranger's invitation, unopened letter, heart's Godot.
Surround yourself with your life but don't
look now. Don't you see? If R. were here
before me, we'd both be disappointed.

   —*So, you stayed.*
                    —*So, you came back.*

Missing Person

Why, like a regretful mother,
unchained ghost, do I hover
over old photos when I'm home
for Christmas or Thanksgiving,
as if I'd all along been living

behind this time-lapse looking glass
I like to think of as my past.
Like to? But I was there, that's me
threading the hook with the worm,
me feeding cake off a knife to a groom

so sweetly, as if he were my own.
He was! Numb as a new clone,
I stare—she does—stunned, stunned:
she, to see that I appear
alone; me, to see her there

without a clue to what's all wrong
with the picture. Glaring, then gone
by the album's final blank pages,
what was missing or too much
there. I seem to need to catch

a spark of knowing in that eye,
opaque as a grape. She thinks I
will approve, imagines me the anti-
climactic aging matron of her
future: a beaming, wistful blur.

I *am* a blur. At least I'm not
what any camera I know has caught.
In albums, on the walls, on the fridges
of friends, you can easily see it.
I've modeled myself like clothes that don't fit.

If you knew me you'd want seconds—
twins, quintuplets! There must be records
of my self-most self. Who knows?
The FBI may classify the files
holding one of my rare true smiles.

If only I could blow up corners
of snapshots taken by foreigners
where I have candidly intruded:
say at sunset, Nantucket pier,
blocking a darling Arsenio's ear

or side by side with a Yoshiko
at Pagsanjan! There I know
the truth of who I am and was
would coincide. Me with my mother
laughing beside some Sasha or other

in Paris. Me with a serious smile
on a bench in Philadelphia, while
Wolfgang cavorts in the foreground
with Helga—photos to confirm
glimpses of being that conform

to the credible evolution of what's
really become of me. So what
if all the negatives are lost?
I know they're out there, fading
somewhere, my hairdo and dress outdating,

but not my earnest, softened gaze
as one of your hands touched my face
and our two shadows between us
fused darkly in the piazza at noon
just beyond Dieter or Hans, that June.

The Next Stop Stopping

Half the luxury in a long train ride
is the reckless notion, nurtured partly
by the rocking, rocking, rocking of the car,
that you could just get out anywhere,
even here, like Lambert Strether
stepping out at last beyond Paris, beyond
the bounds of his conscience (but only
to find himself, as he would say, "deeper in"),
taking a train somewhere past the banlieux
on a sweet-scented summer day, watching
for the first unselfconsciously quaint town
with the right kind of shade trees,
perhaps a lake. An inn beside the lake.
Although it's January now, and chilly
sitting at the window past which everything
takes place, you still play your little game:
Next stop, maybe. There you might unwrap
in some tastefully overstuffed room
whose fireplace is so capaciously ablaze
you can't help thinking *hearth* — aloud —
and though you can hear the other guests
gather murmurously in the adjoining room
you still can't tear yourself from the window
which gives out over a snow-encrusted creek
and a powdered wood whose pines shrug
darkly in the wind, majestically accepting
what whiteness still falls to their limbs . . .

You're inside the train, and it's not snowing now.
An afternoon lined with spindly black trees
bisecting the telephone wires, reminding you
grimly, grimly, grimly, of where you're headed
at this juncture—wedding, trial, interview,
wake—just imagine getting out of it!
Get out and start up something sane and spicy
with a woman, say she owns a local coffee shop,
maybe that's her with the hair, there, that Audi
in the station parking lot, idling patiently
for someone who hasn't gotten there first.
She might have good music on tape, she's
cocking her head to listen, and you're leaving,
or the stop is leaving. After three hours
the train no longer seems to move at all;
each stop itself slows down, pulls up—
not Dickinson's death, but a whole new life
you might try on—and then pulls out
and chugs away, while you get weaker,
increasingly weak with each fresh sacrifice
while all the promising land in between
skates past the window the way it does
on movie sets, projected behind the actors'
stationary heads. Cary Grant, still himself,
and Eva Marie Saint, their only real movement
in their lips, and Eva's hand on the back
of Cary's neck. But when they leave the train
everything is different, it doesn't work,
they wind up clinging to the rock-face.
So you don't get out. You don't even stand
and lift your bags down till it's time.

Lover Release Agreement

Against his lip, whose service has been tendered
lavishly to me, I hold no lien.
Here's his heart, which finally has blundered
from my custody. Here's his spleen.
Hereafter let your hair and eyes and breasts
be venue for his daydreams and his nights.
Here are smart things I've said, and all the rest
you'll hear about. Here are all our fights.
Now, whereas I waive rights to his kiss,
the bed you've shared with him has rendered null
his privilege in mine. Know that, and this:
undying love was paid to me in full.
No matter how your pleasures with him shine,
you'll always be comparing them to mine.

Late Elvis

This movie takes us back behind the scenes
with Elvis cutting up, Elvis falling
laughing off his chair and splitting seams.
We wince in our hearts to see him stalling

rehearsal: he can't remember the words, it's hot,
he can't forget who he really isn't
anymore, lost in his flesh, his white fringed suit,
lost in the high collar, which seems to have risen

behind him on its own, to finish him
the way the Beatles' lasting lightning flashed,
and flashed, to darken and diminish him.
Standing on the past tense of the stage, at last

he mustered something in him up to sing.
Then had to catch his breath. The mike went dead
in his king's hand. He grinned and grabbed four more:
When I . . . -teen fifty-six . . . Hello? he said.

Beckett Dead Imagine

for Jan Jonson

I hear of it washing the dishes,
I slosh and slosh this fact
with bits of oatmeal and grayish suds
down the drain. The next day
in a hurry I step over
a man's black coat, or a man,
what might have been
his very corpse, on my way
into the post office
without so much as a pained
look down.

Hours later I feel exotic guilt
to see his image so quickly
and easily eclipsed by stoplights,
shadows, the merest distraction . . .
How can anyone grieve for a public figure?
(—*Nothing public about Sam Beckett.*
— *Who are you to call him Sam!*)
So what if someone you don't know
has spoken to the part of yourself
that has never before responded
to articulation, or to the touch
of anyone? Doesn't that count for knowing?
And he dies.

Three normal days slip by.
I don't mention this to anyone.

On the fourth day, news columns
lengthen their last-minute obits:
Foxrock, illness, insomniac
mother, recluse, Nobel, illness,
Suzanne, illness, Suzanne
dead. Her dead he couldn't
imagine. Then in six months
him too. Him
dead.

Six days and nights after his last,
how patiently I sit through
woebegone lectures on SB's life,
SB's "musical geometries,"
SB's semi-requited love for Joyce.
My applause might be that
of politely dispassionate palms.
My temples have the bronze cool
of a young mortician's.
I hardly blink.

Then the Swedish director gets up,
lithe and cheerful, smiling, telling
anecdotes about directing *Godot*
at San Quentin (it is easy to be fond
of this blond accent, this European,
voluble divine) and the months
of surprisingly earnest rehearsal
with death-row prisoners
who understood the play better
than anyone on the outside could.
We gaze and gaze at him
whose hands Beckett once
clutched awkwardly to his breast.
Watching his eyes move in memory
to Beckett's eyes I am permitted
to see them too, even in a sense
to be seen . . .

We all lean forward,
some with eyes shining a little
when he remembers explaining to Beckett
about the twelve cancelled performances:
The prisoners escaped before the second act!
We laugh, and laugh again to hear our Swede
mimic Sam's *Ahhh-?* as the cigar
fell from his open mouth
to his untouched demitasse

and Beckett is laughing too now,
now falling silent and then off
laughing helpless again,
"on off, up down, like that,
for twenty minutes.
I never saw anything like."
And the room is swept with it,
the kind of laughter that affects
motor control *(Escaped!)*, a laugh
vibrating intact and alive from his throat
to our Swede's, surviving these years
so we'd laugh hard enough
to mourn him.

We no longer see our Swede clearly,
but the swimming image superimposed
of a taller man, gaunt and wary, sharp-eyed.
(Escaped!) Our Swede may have nine sons
six daughters and three wives,
he will never be so cherished as now,
now as he delivers the line
Beckett stopped laughing
once long enough to utter: *Ah,*
they didn't have the courage to wait.

Buffalo Bayou

People tend to look you in the eye here
in Houston, even the killers,
everywhere here so green and spacious
I could think myself back in South Jersey
except for some mangy pot-bellied palms,
and a few retro-natives in boots who drawl
Y'all awta get y'self a gun, and *Don't never
walk at night here,* not even twilight
and especially not near this bayou
in this park where I'm walking slowly
with old Van Morrison, sweet old Van
with whom I grew up, who never knew my name.

But surely I've got time, the sun still squinting
goldly into the sky, birds still fluttering
comfortably about me, not knowing a stranger
when they see one, when my path bottoms into
the predictably unexpected hush, the low-slung
sullen granite precinct of the city
like some sunken downtown, neat gray blocks
only half-humbled, kneeling upright in a row
to something no one here can name aloud,
enjoying the lushest grass in a ten-mile radius
and the quietest paths, and deepest shade.

My old friend Bernice, too far away to call
except for Sundays between the larger bills,
whose very name makes me smile instantly
with grand irreverence, used to walk with me
in a cemetery like this one, needing privacy,
or a sidelong look at this kind of stillness,
to cool our heels on the pumice of another time
thinking, *We remember you who never knew us,*
to take in sweet air and good weed, and laugh
softly at what had already managed to go wrong,

and what still might, and about the early stage
of our friendship before we knew we'd have one,

angling for the same Brazilian exchange student,
João, whom I remember getting to first
and then she the next night, that exchange,
and weeks and years later exchanging notes,
Bernie telling her weird story of his tears
that fell ice-cold to her cheeks as she lay
beneath him in the grass, blindly kissing him
against the chill night air and wondering dazedly
Why on earth, and *How can tears be cold,*
only later to discover what he'd "wept" —
minuscule particles of gray gravel —
still clinging to her hair.
And she insisted his name was Pedro!

Van probably couldn't remember the name
of his brown-eyed girl, if you asked him.
But that's the point, the uncomplicated joy
in generic beloveds: the summer vacation girl,
and the behind-the-stadium-with-you girl,
and the ones Van must have met above the thrum
of his guitar! Ooh la la, the many many ones!
Sha la la la la la la la la la-la dee da . . .
Just like that. Just as I met João (brown eyes)
across a room while I guess Bernice
was fussing with stuff in her purse,
like those incredibly long cigarettes
she used to smoke, Ticonderogas, Saratogas,
as Pedro—João—tangled lovebeams with me
above guitar strings while others sang,
the way I can still hear Van
above these mockingbirds and jays, but not
the large loping man who overtakes me
and passes on ahead.

The last slant of sun visits briefly each stone.
Each doorless edifice with no room inside
for anyone, being each a solid door unto a door
bearing the names and numbers. Some with flowers,
some without. Most without. (For how long?)
Jays bicker and change places in the new shade,
observing no decorum. Why should they?
The lushest grass, the smoothest stone.
And Van is swinging low, slower and lower,
the batteries in my walkman are running down,
the sun too going down, and I feel a settling
in my soul that we all, bird, self, Bernice, man
who might have mugged me and Van,
all are at peace with these receding distortions,
the world seeming to sharpen now even as it fades,
the wooded bayou deepening along with Van's
slowed-down joyous young voice, my own walk
enchanted almost to halting, and all of us wanting
only to lie down in the cold grass and be kissed,
to be kissed with the cold and lasting sorrow
of stone, be finally told our whole names
and how belovedly and exactly how long
we shall have been known by them.

Password

There must be some reason my daily walks
lead me into streets like this
with carved doors that don't open
into homes or businesses or even bars,
but into dim interiors no one ever
enters or leaves. People hurry by
to stare at me, not because I'm a stranger
since I come here all the time,
not because my lips are still half open
with the last thing I'd meant never to say,
not for these letters I keep dropping. They see
something's wrong.
                          Or can they hear it
in the cyclic uncertainty of my gait,
the way I do and don't care
about the cracks, the dog shit,
the puddles that soak my stockings
inside my only shoes left, which wobble
and squeak now, so full of wrong steps.

But what do they hear?
And don't I hear it too when I'm off guard?
I like to think it's a woman behind me,
sighing, almost but not quite wailing;
I know better than to turn and look,
and I turn.

Inside the machine of my life
there's friction, a frozen bearing,
a 24-hour malfunction. I've shut my eyes
while walking, shut them deeply,   ·
and with my fingers pressed them
further shut until they hurt,
the way you'd lean on a reset button.
But there's no stopping this machine,
which turns out not to be for making
cunning useful articles with smooth handles,
not for moving smoothly toward a destination.

Even if I had a destiny I could afford
it wouldn't take me there, not this life,
always steering me to the next brick wall
I can flatten my back against,
down this or that side street after a man
with purposeful stride who almost looks
like someone, who quickly turns the corner
just as I'm about to reach him, then whisks
into mist.

I've had half a mind to lie down
right here on the curb until this thing
either comes right or conks entirely.
Yesterday a mounted policeman pulled up
in front of the post office to tease
the pharmacist's daughter just as I was
pausing there to erase my return address
from a package I needed stamps for,
and his horse, a gorgeous bay, lowered its head
and nudged me softly in the ribs three times—
as if it knew.

So at least it's narrowed down, we're getting
somewhere. Something needs fixing,
or replacing (just keep walking)
something's not right here,
some letter not written
or not received
or at least not in time,
and in the rain, under my leaky umbrella,
and all the words and especially
that one word
blurred.

Delayed Response

The bright green lizard in my living room
was so quiet I might have missed it
but for staring at the closed venetian blinds
where it had sunned itself since noon
like some blithe poolside Dean Martin,
maybe a cocktail drop of dew balanced
at a slant in one sticky hand. A comma-
end of tail and tiny toe extended
below the slat that curved above.
I'd kept the sun out all day long,
trying to work, but mostly staring
at whatever I imagined myself not doing.
Afraid it might dry up and die
like the paper-thin remains of one
found on the floor just days before,
I spent the rest of the afternoon
with an empty mayo jar and lid
leaning gently, aching by millimeters,
to catch him just to set him loose.

First he shot, green rubber band,
down to the coffee table magazines,
ribs visibly pulsing against a photograph
of Marilyn, looking a bit greener
than before, as I spoke long and coaxingly,
and he seemed to listen, intelligently
naked, frail and annoyed. I knelt,
he sprinted. I crawled and called softly,
crooning after him, promising, oh,
lush fern and endless Houston suns,
until he whipped his tail and zipped
into my unanswered correspondence pile
and I despaired.

I placed a saucer with a little water
on a letter from my ex, and beside it
a copy of *Nature Conservancy* bearing
a cheesecake photo of the doe-eyed
freckle-winged regal fritillary.
He beamed out and we were at it again,
this time no jar, no butterflies, no love
letters, nothing but enough cool distance
and cunning to steer him, by zigs and
zags, out away from me and my helplessly
perilous self, my stupid shoes and
crushing slats, slamming windows,
and air-conditioned skyless rooms
(an hour, including the detour
under the big stuffed chair)
while I promised him what I've never
promised anyone before, even when
the words were what were needed most
to hold the visible heart activity
of two together, even in the days
of green pulsing hard between us
like some Desdemona-level migraine,
even when without the words so easily
withheld like water and sunlight
I knew and I knew he knew it too
it was just going to dry up and die.

Four

The Cry

A busy sky: the birds have turned
their scratchy radios up so loud
at different stations, I've discerned
at least a dozen songs around.
There is one more I listen for,
the way a dog suspends his nap
to whump his tail and whine and sigh:
three arcing notes that overlap
in mind (or was it four?) each cry
I can identify, I listen for.
Bull crickets chafe their noon stick-legs
for all the lady crickets' pleasure.
A bit of trailing cobweb snags
the fence that fences off the pasture
I can't cross to listen for
the cry I heard in my mid-youth
that my stick-brain chafes to recall:
anthem for whatever truth
I knew before I knew it all,
when I heard what I listen for—
too vivid to have been designed
by a lonely child's inventive ear
or to leave me, now at dusk, resigned;
so sweet it can compete, each year,
with what I hear. I listen for
what matched the match with World I made
back then. What frightened off that bird
or silences it when I'm here?
Some secret unsworn? An oath?
It used to aim my self-lost cry
straight from that alder tree's tall shade,
and matched me Why for Why, for Why
was all we answered for; for both
served both as query and reply.

North Jersey Farmland, Vile Mood

This hill is solid dirt.
Exhausted pasture shirks
its only chore, spent,
sprawling all wrong
beyond bent fences bent
in disuse. No one works
the slouched brown field.
Birds withhold song:
no seeds, no fruit, no yield
but one grey cloud, sealed,
as if it could contain
any message but rain.
There isn't even wind
up here; the air has held
its breath. Or died. Beyond
the slope, almost unseen:
two trees, a barn, a shack
built by someone back
when someone had to live
a life out here.
I won't stay. I'd leave
right now if I could shake
the thrall of this low mood.
I think: *Grey. Blear.*
If *think*'s the word.

Then, *gold:* a yellow flood
the cloud splits open
like a sack of yolks—
as if it's hoping
I'll resee that shack
into a farmhouse, bold
beneath such sun,
its roof gone scarlet.
   (such a red!)

Trite, narcissistic heart,
you're cheaply sold.
(the little roof is red!)

Before the Sickness Is Official

I bring you a book I've always wanted to read.
I don't think you know yet that I know.
I don't bring photographs.
I don't bring flowers that will die in your azure vase
on the cool marble table.
I don't bring potted plants that will live
a long long time.
I give you a slightly twisted smile
and you give it right back.
Want some wine?
I drink beer instead.
My words come out unwieldy
with the weight of other words.

Everything in your apartment is so clean,
as if you were expecting some other guest.

You bring me the new sketches
which ostensibly I came here to see
and I take your time looking at them.
You take a phone call in the kitchen,
where your voice assumes a new business-
likeness, distant and rehearsed.

I lift a paperweight and put it back
exactly where it was.

You carry your wine back into the room
with your pale, strong-boned fingers.
We compete in cracking the pistachios
that don't have openings, giving points
for neatness of shell and wholeness of nut.
The nuts are in a crimson bowl
you made in ninth grade.
The sketches are inchoate but good.
I tell you they're good.
I tell you they're really good.
You pause and give me a chance to bring it up.
I pause too. I say it's late.
You give me back my coat, its pockets
full of keys to my future car,
my future office, my future apartments
shared with friends I don't yet know.
As I leave, you joke briefly about
your thinning hair: *Parting is such sweet sorrow.*
Then you say something else
I won't be able to recall.

Realism

She wants it all in, the whole all of it,
the clock at precisely 4:40, the shadows
impossibly accurate, the very dust in the air,
the smudge on the knee of my jeans,
every imperfection *mise au point*.
She's my friend so I hold still for her
and her supple sable brushes, the stiff
thin line of her mouth seeming to force
the issue of my exact position versus
hers, sharpening my arm against the wall
I can't see. She's getting the half-moon
of my left thumb, the twisted strap (with
knot) of the worn leather purse slumped
at my right, the curled collar facing,
the eyebrow tilting up and the eyebrow
not, right down to my willfully
unwilling stillness. Nonetheless,
the portrait is much too smiley for me.
I never smile except when she paints me,
because I know her flaws, stubborn bitch,
I know she'll go ahead and paint a smile in.
I figure it may as well be mine.

Late Letter

Just when I think I've gotten past regret
comes this posthumous letter, warmly sent
to murmur *remember,* and whisper *forget*

those days: I'm sorry for the things I said.
And if you can forgive me now, my friend . . . .
Just when you thought you'd gotten past regret

you learned the love you had was not love yet.
The word was sweetest when it wasn't meant.
It murmured *remember.* It whispers *forget.*

You close with a mock-angry epithet.
The rules of love work better when they're bent.
Oh, don't we always think we're past regret

(don't skies perversely bask their bluest yet)
one day before November's wet cement
cries out coldly *remember*, coldly *forget*?

Fever exaggerates the cheeks' last red.
Our blood is at its brightest when it's spent,
just when we think we've gotten past regret.
We murmur *remember.* It whispers *forget.*

Raven

She can't believe this jag-winged majesty
really wants a piece of her small cold life,
godless and cold, and yet it circles her
on shouldery black wings, blacker than dried blood,
now holding still against the sky like a slit
opening into somewhere else, now half-wheeling,
the charred remains of dark thoughts flown . . .

But not gone. It reappears and shadows her,
calling, calling her quick steps weak, weak,
bored and exposed for those of a woman
trying too hard to get lost in the woods,
clearing her throat as if for company,
snapping twigs, pretending to seek—to need—
what mitigated solace there may be
in the leatherish creak of new snow.

It's no use. She can't *get* lost,
can't even fear death with any decency,
seeing there the unmistakable glint
of sun off a window through the landscaped
brace of trees beyond these, these unplanned.
And because beneath her creaking boots
comes the unsoothing hum and wheeze
of not distant traffic, a muffled laughter
at the hungry anachronism overhead.

Oh, she'd like to believe she could die;
it would give her an edge,
a key to open the steely manmade gate
of reason's garden, let her into the wilderness
of fear and belief, where she could really freeze
to death and be eaten quickly by a big
black bird, and die consciously in the snow,
which would begin to feel delicious, like
a slow transfusion of warm sake,
and to taste unspeakably
like the saliva of a hungry god.

Sugar Dada

Go home. It's never what you think it is,
The kiss, the diamond, the slamdance pulse in the wrist.
Nothing is true, my dear, not even this

Glimmer of passion you'll doubtless insist
On perceiving in my glance. Please just
Go. Home is never what you think it is.

Meaning lies in meaning's absence. That mist
Is always almost just about to lift.
Nothing is truer. Dear, not even this

Candle can explain its searing twist
Of flame mounted on cool amethyst.
Go on home—not where you think it is,

But where you would expect its comfort least,
In still-black stars our century will miss
Seeing. Nothingness is not as true as this

Faith we grind up with denial: grist
To the midnight mill; morning's catalyst.
Come, let's go home, wherever you think it is.
Nothing is true, my dear. Not even this.

Sea and Rain

(after Whistler)

The sea alone will do it
if you walk close enough
to lose a few footprints

but do not let your heels
get sucked down
or let yourself think
you can ever make a stand
by the sea in the sand
on a gray day

gray ones being by far
the most effective
and a high spraying wind helps
which the sea generally provides
keening with the smell
of struggling unseeable fish

while the salt-embalming sound
of wind and moon and sand
siphons direct to inner ear
as if from inside like the swish
and yawning roar of the womb
you are not supposed to recall
barely beneath which underfoot
you hear the sound of shells
unfleshed and pounded to nothing
moons and moons ago
hissing up now no reason

pounded and crushed and shushed

and then that gasp
forced out of you
when a gust shoves too much
air down your throat
like a soft innocent fist
so you can't breathe
though you can't be said
not to breathe

you being by now blended
into this horizonless
sea sky sand of brown-gray
(like your hair and hands)
reflecting blue (like
veins under skin) under
blue-gray-brown with white
(scarf blown away)
under white-gray-blue-brown

the senses all pounded smooth
numbing even as they quicken
for sharp gagging breaths you take
to remember you are
not this you are absolutely nothing
like the indiscriminate swash
of sparkling deadness and darkened life
thronging at you here

then a few drops of rain

a few more

you are not nothing
or if you are
you at least almost know it
and can keep walking

The Brain of the World

Predawn: my forehead half against the glass.
What I begin to see cannot be meant
for any passenger. They're all asleep.
Even the pilot has passed out, whose last
crackle I half-heard: . . . *ask that you keep*
your seatbelts . . . one hell of a headwind . . .
Something vaguely thickening below.
This is no mere cloud, this vastly furled
unfurling. There is no ocean so intricate,
so fissured, coiled with attentiveness.
It looks like a brain. It must be the brain of the world
we've stumbled on, one firmament too high—
I'm almost embarrassed to look. It's all here:
the soft, mussed angel hair of the frontal lobe
we move smoothly over like a laser probe
above and between one burgeoned hemisphere
and the other, with a view of everything:
a PET scan darkly limning the history
of all progress, regress, beauty, pain,
more pain: we drift above the hypothalamus
too long. One mystery lump
in its oatmeal glows for a moment.
Could this be the pineal gland, tiny germ
said to entangle body and mind?

I don't want to see this stuff,
its sticky gray fibers luminously secret,
like the insulation lining an attic
one was warned away from as a child—
and no wonder, its boxes unbearable,
weighted with the dross of passions:
triumphal bric-a-brac, uniforms,
wedding dresses, the terrible headless
soldiers and horses with missing legs,

one black pawn and two white bishops,
rubber masks like burnt flesh, dried chips
of wings of bees, maps with obsolete borders,
a scotch-taped lock of someone's hair;
the vanity of relics man-begotten
and -begone, battened, packed
like slightly soiled cotton balls
into a fixed jostle of image and emblem
wrapped and ready to flash out seriatim
like the memories of the near-dead man
on last night's news who, clinging
to the windshield of his stolen car, going
ninety, saw what all the near-dead see:
every woman, man and thing he'd ever
cared about—and some he really hadn't—
filed before his wind-whipped eyes.

I wish I could sleep, but now it's beginning
to look like old gefilte fish, the moistly flattened
convolutions deeper, an old amygdala
stressed by oilings of the seas, blackened
albatross and struggling gull, the shifting
of ancient rivers, the drowning of crops,
the thrones of evil and the ovens; welts
of women and slaves; and here, a coal-edged hole,
as if a bomb or overheated sunset singed it;
and there, the curved mark famine left,
like the patches and cracks in droughty earth.
Here are fuzzy turrets of art; the carvings
of cavemen, the reckless inking of romance,
the stark ravings of poet after poet blaming
the cravings of the spirit on the craven
body of the world. Here lies a vortex
of silver, bearing the noble evolution
of the Least Flycatcher. Now a vaster stretch
of slatey ooze—the limbic wash of the cortex
lamenting torn ozone, and whole countries

left to starve; and every last rib-bone
of those with souls gone all to hell, or just gone.

How can the world stand it? The memory
of so much wrong and right, come and gone
and still going to come, again to go.
Farther on, the agitated pinkish tufts
of hippocampus, inflamed beyond
repair: memory and meaning stricken
with each new perception.

So *that's* it.
The world stores all, remembers nothing.
That's its secret! That's how it survives.

Suddenly its mute gray pulse revolts me,
its sentience only reflex, limited to here, to now:
a temporal vacuum. Only the present
is the world, and the world is only present.
Like the post-encephalitic who rises
to greet his wife with a joy near tears:
two minutes later he looks at a table or chair,
and turning back—*Darling! Darling, can it be you?*—
sees her again for the first time in years.

When I wake, my pillow is in place,
the flight attendant's offering orange
or tomato juice. A notebook
lies open on my lap.
The sun streams in, shining and shining.

CRAB ORCHARD AWARD SERIES IN POETRY